Building Mount Rushmore

Alicia Z. Klepeis

Cavendish
Square

New York

Published in 2018 by Cavendish Square Publishing, LLC
243 5th Avenue, Suite 136, New York, NY 10016

Library of Congress Cataloging-in-Publication Data

Names: Klepeis, Alicia, 1971- author.
Title: Building Mount Rushmore / Alicia Z. Klepeis.
Description: New York : Cavendish Square Publishing, 2018. | Series: Engineering North America's landmarks | Includes bibliographical references and index.
Identifiers: LCCN 2017013874 (print) | LCCN 2017017651 (ebook) | ISBN 9781502629555 (E-book) | ISBN 9781502629548 (library bound) | ISBN 9781502629524 (pbk.) | ISBN 9781502629531 (6 pack)
Subjects: LCSH: Mount Rushmore National Memorial (S.D.)--Juvenile literature.
Classification: LCC F657.R8 (ebook) | LCC F657.R8 K54 2018 (print) | DDC 978.3/93--dc23
LC record available at https://lccn.loc.gov/2017013874

Editorial Director: David McNamara
Editor: Fletcher Doyle
Copy Editor: Rebecca Rohan
Associate Art Director: Amy Greenan
Designer: Alan Sliwinski
Production Coordinator: Karol Szymczuk
Photo Research: J8 Media

Printed in the United States of America

Contents

The Confederate Memorial Carving is on Stone Mountain near Atlanta, Georgia.

Chapter One

An Idea Comes to Life

The year was 1923. South Dakota had been a state for thirty-four years. Beautiful South Dakota did not draw many visitors. Why not? In the 1920s, getting to South Dakota was hard. There were no highways. There were no airports.

Doane Robinson was the state historian. He had a vision. Robinson heard about the work of Gutzon Borglum. Borglum was a sculptor. In 1923, he was creating a sculpture of Robert E. Lee in

This portrait of historian Doane Robinson was taken in 1928.

Georgia. Borglum was **carving** this sculpture into Stone Mountain.

Robinson wanted people to visit South Dakota. He wanted people to come from all over the United States. Robinson heard that many people were driving to visit Borglum's work. Maybe people would drive to see a sculpture in South Dakota, too.

An Invitation and Two Trips

In August 1924, Robinson wrote a letter inviting Borglum to South Dakota. Borglum visited the Black

Hills twice with his twelve-year-old son, Lincoln. During the second trip, the sculptor found his "canvas." Gutzon Borglum chose Mount Rushmore for his famous sculpture in August 1925.

This was what Mount Rushmore looked like in August 1927. This was before carving began. The lines on the rocks mark placements for the presidents.

Gutzon Borglum works on George Washington's head in his Mount Rushmore studio. There is a scale model of the memorial on the right.

Doane Robinson imagined a huge sculpture in the Black Hills. He suggested Western heroes.

Borglum felt it was better to **carve** national heroes into Mount Rushmore. He wanted presidents to represent the country's history. He picked George Washington, Thomas Jefferson, Abraham Lincoln, and Theodore Roosevelt.

George Washington was the nation's first president. Thomas Jefferson made the Louisiana Purchase. This doubled the size of the country. Abraham Lincoln ended slavery and kept the country together. Theodore Roosevelt created many national parks and national monuments.

Fast Fact

South Dakota Senator Peter Norbeck (left) repeatedly raised money for the monument so that it could be completed.

Mount Rushmore by the Numbers

Length of Construction: More than fourteen years (October 4, 1927, to October 31, 1941).

Cost of Construction: $989,992, or about $16 million in today's money.

Weird statistic: George Washington's nose is 21 feet (6.4 meters) long. That's about 1 foot (0.3 m) longer than the other presidents' noses on Mount Rushmore.

Workers on the project: About four hundred in total. There were typically thirty men on the mountain at any one time.

Mountain Maintenance: Every year, repairs are made to prevent cracks from damaging the site. Trained mountain climbers use a silicone **caulk** to seal tiny cracks before they grow.

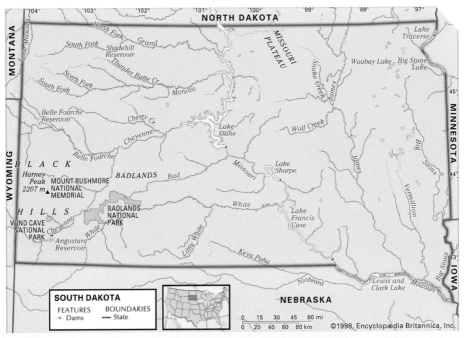

This map of South Dakota shows the state's national parks, lakes, and other physical features. Mount Rushmore is in the southwest.

Two men use a winch to lower workers from the top of Mount Rushmore.

Chapter Two

Problems Crop Up

Carving Mount Rushmore required skill and teamwork. It also needed heavy equipment, technology, and lots of **dynamite**. There were many problems to fix. One was getting people to the work site.

Each morning, the workers climbed hundreds of stairs to get up the mountain. **Winches** then lowered the men to their work spots. They hung in the air held by a **harness** in a **bosun** chair. Cables attached the bosun chair to the winch. The harness

Sitting in a bosun chair, Gutzon Borglum inspects work being done on the memorial.

was buckled around the worker's waist. Men could sit safely in them and move side to side. Their hands were free to work.

Math, Models, and Mountains

Borglum made plaster models of the presidents in his studio. The figures he would carve into the mountain were twelve times bigger than the models. So each inch on the model would be 12 inches (30.5 centimeters) on the mountain. Each foot would be equal to 12 feet (3.7 m).

The head of each model was 5 feet (1.5 m) tall. So each head on the mountain face would be 60 feet (18.3 m) high.

How did the team get the measurements from the models to the mountain? Borglum came up with a clever way to do the job.

Borglum's Pointing Machine

How did the sculptor figure out exactly where to put Abraham Lincoln's nose? He made a special pointing machine. His pointing machine measured three distances. From a fixed spot it measured length in a straight line. This told him how far out the end of Lincoln's nose should be. The machine measured angles right to left. This told him where the sides of Lincoln's nose should be. And it

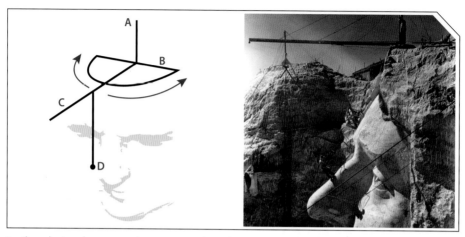

In the photo above, workmen are using the pointing machine. The drawing shows the parts of the machine. There is the pole to set a fixed point (A), the protractor at the base (B), the pole to measure angles and distance from the fixed point (C), and the line that measures vertical distance from the base (D).

measured up and down. This told him where the top and bottom of the nose should be.

A small pointing machine was placed on the models. A large pointing machine was placed on the top of each president's head. First, the model was measured. Let's say the distance from the pointing machine to the top of his nose was

20 inches (0.5 m). Multiply 20 inches by 12 inches to get 240 inches (20 × 12 = 240). That equals 20 feet (6 m). The top of the nose on the mountain should be 20 feet down from the pointing machine.

Men known as pointers put all of the measurement points from the models onto the mountain. These points told the carvers where to cut. All they had to do was connect the dots.

This photo, taken around 1935, shows dynamite blasting rock away from the face of Abraham Lincoln.

Fast Fact

Ninety percent of Mount Rushmore was carved using dynamite. Before the men could use jackhammers or chisels to sculpt the faces, they had to blow up over 450,000 tons (408,233 metric tons) of rock!

Stone Setbacks

The stone was Mount Rushmore's biggest problem. Some of the **granite** was weak. It was not strong enough to support the sculpture.

Before Borglum's workers could **chisel** anything, they had to reach sturdy stone. How did they do this? Dynamite. Drillers would make holes in the granite. Workers known as powder monkeys placed dynamite in the holes. They used just enough to blast away only weak stone.

The Protractor

The base of Borglum's pointing machine was a protractor. A protractor measures angles in degrees. There are 360 degrees in each circle. There are 180 degrees in each half circle. If you stand with your arms straight out from your sides, your left hand points to 0 degrees. Your right hand points to 180 degrees. If you look straight ahead, your nose points to 90 degrees. A pole on the protractor could swing like a needle on a dial. It moved left to right to degree marks on the protractor. Degrees on the model are the same as degrees on the mountain.

Mount Rushmore workmen pose for a photo at the base of the mountain.

Chapter Three

One for the Ages

Building Mount Rushmore wasn't easy. Also, it was not quick. It took fourteen years to complete this incredible carving. Turning a mountain into a work of art had never been done on a **scale** like this.

Borglum and his team worked hard to bring four US presidents to life in stone. It took hundreds of men to build the monument. Every man had a role. Some blasted the stone away with dynamite. Others used drills. Still other men used

Stone workers use air hammers to carve the eyes of Thomas Jefferson. The workers are standing on scaffolding.

bumping hammers. These tools made the stone smooth.

The work was tough. Men had to hold drill **bits** in awkward positions as they chipped away at the rock. Stone dust covered their faces and clothes. Some days were freezing cold. Others were very hot. Yet, the men never gave up. They knew how important this project was.

Unhappy times came often at Mount Rushmore. When money ran out, workers couldn't be paid.

Work stopped. No work was done in 1928. Out of the fourteen years of the project, workers spent about six and a half years carving. The other time was lost to money and weather problems.

Some of the project's problems had to do with Borglum himself. He had a bad temper and was tough to work for. Borglum fired workers when he got angry. His son, Lincoln, often smoothed things over and hired them back.

Problem Presidents

Borglum's team had the most trouble carving Thomas Jefferson. The rock where Jefferson was meant to be carved was too soft. Workers tried that spot for eighteen months. Finally Borglum had to make a change. He had workmen blast away all

Thomas Jefferson was supposed to be to George Washington's right. Bad rock caused a change in plans. Jefferson was recarved on Washington's left.

that had been done on Jefferson. Then they started over on the other side of George Washington.

Theodore Roosevelt's head was also not exactly where Borglum had planned. The workers had to go back 80 feet (24 m) from the mountain face to

find solid enough rock
for carving.

Legacy of Mount Rushmore

Mount Rushmore
is one of America's
most popular tourist
attractions. Why? This
mountain is special.
It depicts some of
the most important

Gutzon Borglum talks with some of his stone workers while inspecting the eye of one of the presidents.

leaders in our nation's history. Some call Mount
Rushmore a monument to democracy.

Doane Robinson wanted Mount Rushmore
carved to bring people to South Dakota.

Peter Norbeck helped select a beautiful route to get people to Mount Rushmore. It's called Iron Mountain Road. It was built in the 1930s.

More than three million people visit Mount Rushmore every year. They come from all fifty states and countries around the globe. The words of President Calvin Coolidge are still fitting: "This memorial will crown the height of land between the Rocky Mountains and the Atlantic Seaboard, where coming generations may view it for all time."

World's Largest Stone Carvings

1. God of Longevity In China's Meng Shan Mountains, it is 715 feet (218 m) high and 656 feet (200 m) wide.

2. Crazy Horse Memorial In the Black Hills, it will be 563 feet (171.6 m) high and 641 feet (195.4 m) long when it is done.

3. Leshan Giant Buddha In a cliff face in China, it is 233 feet (71 m) high.

4. Bamiyan Buddhas Ruined in Afghanistan, they stood 180 feet (54.9 m) and 120 feet (36.6 m) high.

5. Statue of Decebalus Romania's King Decebalus stands 131 feet (40 m).

Mount Rushmore Quiz

1. How long did it take to carve the mountain?

2. In what state is Mount Rushmore located?

3. Which presidents are depicted on the memorial?

4. How many people visit the site each year?

Answers

1. Fourteen years.

2. South Dakota.

3. George Washington, Abraham Lincoln, Thomas Jefferson, and Theodore Roosevelt.

4. Three million.

📍 Glossary

bit The cutting part of a tool.

bosun An officer on a ship in charge of equipment and the hull. He hung in a bosun chair to fix the ship's hull.

bumping hammer A small, air-powered hammer used for smoothing the surface of a sculpture.

carve To make a shape by cutting a hard material like rock.

caulk A waterproof filler used to repair building cracks.

chisel A metal tool that has a cutting edge at the end of a blade. It is used to chip away at wood or stone.

dynamite A very powerful explosive.

granite A very hard type of rock that can be used for buildings, statues, and countertops.

harness A safety system of belts and straps.

scale A size or a proportion between measurements.

winch A machine that winds a cable or rope around a cylinder so it can go up or down.

⚲ Find Out More

Books

Falk, Laine. *What Is Mount Rushmore?* New York: Scholastic, Inc., 2009.

Gunderson, Jessica. *Mount Rushmore: Myths, Legends, and Facts*. North Mankato, MN: Capstone Press, 2015.

Kelley, True. *Where Is Mount Rushmore?* New York: Grosset & Dunlap, 2015.

Websites

Mount Rushmore

http://www.history.com/topics/us-presidents/mount-rushmore

This History Channel page includes articles, photos, and videos that tell the history of Mount Rushmore.

Mount Rushmore National Memorial

https://www.mtrushmorenationalmemorial.com

The memorial's official website provides information on planning a trip to Mount Rushmore.

Index

Page numbers in **boldface** are illustrations. Entries in **boldface** are glossary terms.

About the Author

Alicia Z. Klepeis began her career at the National Geographic Society. She is the author of numerous children's books including *Trolls*, *Haunted Cemeteries Around The World*, and *A Time For Change*. Alicia visited Mount Rushmore as a child and hopes to go back someday.